T0065875

THE KING'S SINGERS
CHRISTMAS SONGBOOK

EIGHT ARRANGEMENTS FROM THE 2016 ALBUM

ISBN 978-1-4950-7775-3

Visit Hal Leonard Online at
www.halleonard.com

INTRODUCTION

Christmas has always been a very special time of year for The King's Singers. With our heritage firmly rooted in King's College in Cambridge, the annual Service of Nine Lessons and Carols and its worldwide broadcast on Christmas Eve remains an important part of our identity. We enjoy putting together our own special Christmas concert programmes every year that blend traditional carols of the past with newly-imagined nativity pieces and contemporary close harmony arrangements.

This collection of new arrangements, envisaged as a companion to *The King's Singers Christmas Songbook*, brings together a selection of ancient and modern carols and songs that conjure up the magic of this special time of year – all arranged by Berty Rice and Keith Roberts, two former members of the world-famous choir at King's College, Cambridge. Whether you want a carol for church, a pop song for a school concert or just to join with friends around the piano during the holiday season, we hope you enjoy adding a little bit of King's Singers Christmas spirit to your own celebrations!

– *The King's Singers*

DING DONG! MERRILY ON HIGH

For SATBBB a cappella

Duration: ca. 2:20

Words by
GEORGE RATCLIFFE WOODWARD

Traditional French Tune
Arranged by ROBERT RICE

5
mf
S
Ding dong! Mer-ri-ly on high, in heav'n the bells are ring - ing.
A
ding,
T
ding, Mer-ri-ly on high, in heav'n the bells are ring-ing.
B 1
ding, the bells are
B 2
ding, the bells are
B
ding,
5
S
Ding dong! Ver-i-ly the sky is riv'n with an-gels sing - ing,
A
Ding dong ding! The sky is riv'n with an-gels sing -
T
Ding dong! Ver-i-ly the sky is riv'n with an-gels sing-ing,
B 1
ring - ing.
B 2
ring - ing.
B
Ding dong! Ver-i-ly the sky is riv'n with an-gels sing-ing,
9

13
S
A
T
B 1
B 2
B
mp
ing,
Glo - - -
Glo - - -
Glo - ri - a, glo - ri - a, glo - ri - a, glo - ri -
13
- - ri - a! Ho - san - na in ex - cel - sis!
- - ri - a! Ho - san - na in ex - cel - sis!
a, glo - ri - a, glo - ri - a! Ho - san - na in ex - cel - sis!
p
cresc.
17

21
S
A
T
B 1
B 2
B
Glo - - -
ri - a! Ho - san - na in ex - cel - sis!
25

29
S
A
T
B 1
B 2
B
p
Ding dong ding dong ding dong ding dong ding dong
Ding dong ding dong ding dong ding dong ding
Ding dong ding dong ding dong ding dong
Ding dong ding dong ding dong ding dong ding dong
Ding dong ding dong ding dong ding ding,
Ding dong ding dong
33
mf
ding,
ding, let bells be
ding,
ding, let bells be
E'en so here be-low, be - low, let stee - ple bells be swung - en,
ding, here be-low, be-low, let stee - ple bells be swung - en,

S
A
T
B 1
B 2
B
mf
And "I - o, i - o, i - o" by peo - ple sung - en.
swung - en,
mf
and peo - ple
swung - en, And "I - o, i - o, i - o" by priest and peo - ple
And "I - o, i - o, i - o" by priest and peo - ple sung - en.
And "I - o, i - o, i - o" by priest and peo - ple sung - en.
37
41
Glo - - -
Glo - - -
sung - en. Glo - ri - a, glo - ri - a, glo - ri - a, glo - ri -
sung - en.
41
41

S
A
T
B 1
B 2
B
ri - a! Ho - san - na in ex - cel - sis!
ri - a! Ho - san - na in ex - cel - sis!
a, glo - ri - a, glo - ri - a! Ho - san - na in ex - cel - sis! Glo -
45
49
Glo
49

S
- - ri - a! Ho - san - na in ex - cel - sis!
A
- - ri - a! Ho - san - na in ex - cel - sis!
T
- - ri - a! Ho - san - na in ex - cel - sis!
B 1
- - ri - a! Ho - san - na in ex - cel - sis!
B 2
- - ri - a! Ho - san - na in ex - cel - sis!
B
- - ri - a! Ho - san - na in ex - cel - sis!
p
53
57
S
Ding dong ding dong ding dong ding dong ding dong,
A
Ding dong ding dong ding dong ding dong ding dong,
T
Ding dong ding dong ding dong ding dong,
B 1
Ding dong ding dong ding dong ding dong ding dong,
B 2
Ding dong ding dong ding dong ding ding,
B
Ding dong ding dong,
57
57

61
S
A
T
B 1
B 2
B
mf
Pray you, du - ti - ful - ly prime your ma - tin chime, ye ring - ers.
Ding dong ding dong ding dong ding dong ding dong,
Ding ding dong ding dong ding dong ding dong
Ding dong ding dong ding dong ding dong ding dong
Ding dong ding dong ding dong ding ding
Ding dong ding dong
May you beau - ti - ful - ly rhyme your eve - time song, ye sing - ers.
May you beau - ti - ful - ly rhyme your eve - time song, ye sing - ers.
ding, May you beau - ti - ful - ly rhyme your eve - time song, ye sing - ers.
ding dong, May you rhyme your eve - time song, ye sing - ers.
dong ding dong, May you rhyme your eve - time song, ye sing - ers.
ding dong ding, May you rhyme your eve - time song, ye sing - ers.
65

69
S
Glo -
A
Glo -
T
Glo - ri - a, glo - ri -
B 1
Glo - -
B 2
Glo - -
B
Glo - ri - a, glo - ri - a!
69
69
S
-
(o) -
A
-
(o) -
T
a!
Glo - ri - a, glo - ri -
B 1
(o) - -
B 2
(o) - -
B
Glo - ri - a, glo - ri - a!
73

77
S
A
T
B 1
B 2
B
mf
mp
f
(o) - ri - a!
(o) - ri - a!
a! Glo - ri - a, glo - ri - a!
(o) - ri - a! Ho -
(o) - ri - a! Ho -
Glo - ri - a, glo - ri - a! Ho -
Ho - san - na in ex - cel - sis!
Ho - san - na in ex - cel - sis!
Ho - san - na in ex - cel - sis!
san - na in ex - cel - sis, in ex - cel - sis!
san - na in ex - cel - sis, in ex - cel - sis!
san - na in ex - cel - sis, ex - cel - sis!
81

85
S
Glo - - -
A
Glo - - -
T
Glo - - -
B 1
Glo - - -
B 2
Glo - - -
B
Glo - - -
85
85
S
- - ri - a! in ex - cel - sis!
A
- - ri - a! in ex - cel - sis!
T
- - ri - a! in ex - cel - sis!
B 1
- - ri - a! Ho - san - na in ex - cel - sis!
B 2
- - ri - a! in ex - cel - sis!
B
- - ri - a! Ho - san - na in ex - cel - sis!
89

93
S
A
T
B 1
B 2
B
ff
Glo - - -
93
ff
- - ri - a!
- - ri - a! Ho - san - na in ex -
- - ri - a! Ho - san - na in ex -
- - ri - a! Ho - san - na in ex -
- - ri - a! Ho - san - na in ex -
- - ri - a! Ho - san - na in ex -
99
mf
mp
sub. mp
97

S
A
T
B 1
B 2
B
cel - sis, Ho - san - na in ex -
cel - sis, ex - cel - sis, Ho - san - na, ho - san - na in ex -
cel - sis, in ex - cel - sis, Ho - san - na, ho -
cel - sis, ex - cel - sis, Ho - san - na, ho - san - na in ex -
cel - sis, Ho - san - na in ex - cel - sis,
cel - sis, Ho - san - na,
101
cel - sis, Ho - san - na in ex - cel - sis!
cel - sis, ex - cel - sis, Ho - san - na in ex - cel - sis!
san - na in ex - cel - sis, Ho - san - na in ex - cel - sis!
cel - sis, ex - cel - sis, Ho - san - na in ex - cel - sis!
Ho - san - na, ho - san - na in ex - cel - sis!
ho - san - na in ex - cel - sis!
marcato
div.
(senza rit.)
105

FROSTY VS. RUDOLPH: THE RE-BOOT

For SATBBB a cappella

Duration: ca. 3:40

Arranged by ROBERT RICE

S
A
T
B 1
B 2
B
mf
of Ru-dolph the Red-nosed Rein-deer,
the Red-nosed Rein-deer,
Ah the Red-nosed Rein-deer,
Ah
cor-po-rat-ing de-tails, Ah and his
3
rit.
a matt-nosed rein-deer world.
ad lib.
bat-tle for ac-cept-ance, in a matt-nosed rein-deer world.
5

7 With excitement and fun (♩ = ca. 104)
S A
T
B 1 B 2
B
talk - in' 'bout
Frost - y the Snow - man, with Ru - dolph still to go,
Frost - y the Snow - man, with Ru - dolph still to go,
Ding ding a ching a d ding ding a ching ding ding a ching a d ding
7 With excitement and fun (♩ = ca. 104)
Alto only
Frost - y, he rocked out in the snow.
Frost - y the Snow - man, he rocked out in the snow.
Frost - y the Snow - man, he rocked out in the snow.
ding ding a ching a d ding ding a ching, he rocked out in the snow and he threw shapes.

11
FROSTY THE SNOW MAN
Words and Music by STEVE NELSON and JACK ROLLINS
S
A
T
B 1
B 2
B
p
mf
mp
Ding ding ching a ding_ ding a ching ding ding ching a ding_
Frost - y the Snow - man_ was a jol - ly hap - py soul,_ with a
Ding ding ching a ding_ ding a ching ding ding ching a ding_
Frost - y, yes, I'm talk - in' 'bout Frost - y, what a snow - dude.
11
ding ding ching a ding_ ding a ching ding ding ching a ding_ ding a ching
corn - cob pipe and a but - ton nose_ and two eyes made out of coal._
ding ding ching a ding_ ding a ching ding ding ching a ding_ ding a ching
Ding ding ching a ding_ ding a ching ding ding ching a ding_ ding a ching
13

T
B 1
B 2
B
ding ding ching a ding ding a ching ding ding ching a ding
Frost - y the Snow - man is a fair - y tale they say, he was
ding ding ching a ding ding a ching ding ding ching a ding
mp
Yes, I'm talk-in' 'bout Frost - y, well, they say, Dm
15
mp
unis.
doo doo doo doo, came to life one day. There
mp
made of snow, but the chil-dren know how he came to life one day. There
mp
doo doo doo doo, came to life one day. There
dm tsm dm tsm dm tsm dm tsm, came to life one mag - i - cal day.
mp
17

19
S
A
T
B 1
B 2
B
must have been some mag - ic in that old silk hat they found, for
must have been some mag - ic in that old silk hat they found, for
must have been some mag - ic in that old silk hat they found, for
must have been some mag - ic in that old silk hat they found, for
19
19
mf
f
when, on, da - da - dance a-round, yeah.
when they placed it on his head he be - gan to dance a-round, yeah.
when, on, da - da - dance a-round, yeah.
unis.
when, on, be-gan to dance a-round, yeah.
21

24 Swing! (♩ = ca. 140)
Frost - y the Snow - man was a - live as he could be,
Frost - y the Snow - man was a - live, a - live as
Frost - y the Snow - man was a - live, a - live as
Frost - y the Snow - man was a - live, a - live as
Dm tsm dm ts dm b tsm dm tsm dm tsm dm tsm
he could be, and the chil - dren say he could laugh and play just the
he could be, and the chil - dren say he could laugh and play just the
he could be, and the chil - dren say he could laugh and play just the
dm ts dm b tsm dm tsm dm tsm dm tsm dm tsm

S A
T
B 1 B 2
B
unis.
32
mp
same as you and me.
Oo,
mf
dm tsm dm tsm dm tsm dm,
Ru - dolph the bold,
30
Ru - dolph of old,
with his pro - bos - cis bright, Hi!
33

RUDOLPH THE RED-NOSED REINDEER

Music and Lyrics by JOHNNY MARKS

44
unis. mf
unis.
S A
All of the oth - er rein - deer used to laugh and call him names,
T
All of the oth - er rein - deer rude - ly used to laugh and call him names,
B 1
All of the oth - er rein - deer rude - ly used to laugh and call him names, (Poor Ru - dolph!)
B 2
All of the oth - er rein - deer used to laugh and call him names,
B
dm dm b dm dm dm dm dm dm b dm dm dm b dm b
44
they nev - er let poor Ru - dolph join in an - y rein - deer games.
Oh, poor Ru - dy could - n't join in an - y rein - deer games. Oo
Oh, poor Ru - dy could - n't join in an - y rein - deer games. Oo
Oh, poor Ru - dy could - n't join in an - y rein - deer games.
dm b dm b dm b dm
E - ven his fa - vour - ites.
48

52
unis. mf
Then one fog - gy Christ - mas eve, San - ta came to say,
p
Oo
p
Oo
52
p
S
A
T
B 1
B 2
B
p
unis.
Doo doo doo doo
Doo doo doo doo
Doo doo doo doo
mf
"Ru - dolph, with your nose so bright, won't you guide my
Doo doo doo doo
56

S A
T
B 1
B 2
B
unis. f
doo, "Oh, ho ho ho ho." Well,
f
doo, "Oh, ho ho ho ho." Well,
f
doo, "Oh, ho ho ho ho." Well,
sleigh to - night?"
f
doo, "Oh, ho ho ho ho." Well,
f
59
62
mf
then they cried, "Hey, Ru - dy!" Da da da
mf
then they cried, "Hey Ru - dy!" Da da da
mf
then they cried, "Hey Ru - dy!" Da da da
f
Then all the rein - deer loved him as they shout - ed out with
mf
Doo doo doo doo doo doo
62
mf
62

S
A
T
B 1
B 2
B
da, shout - ed out with glee: "Ru - dolph,
da, shout - ed out with glee: "Ru - dolph,
da, shout - ed out with glee: "Ru - dolph,
glee: "Ru - dolph the Red - nosed Rein - deer,
doo doo doo doo doo doo
65
With excitement and fun (♩ = ca. 104) (even 8ths)
you'll go down in his - to - ry!"
you'll go down in his - to - ry!"
you'll go down in his - to - ry!"
you'll go down in his - to - ry!"
subito "Frosty" tempo
doo doo dm dm dm dm, Ding ding ching a ding a ding ching
With excitement and fun (♩ = ca. 104) (even 8ths)
68

71
S
A
T
B 1
B 2
B
p
talk - in' 'bout
Frost - y the Snow - man, with Ru - dolph's sto - ry done,
Frost - y the Snow - man, with Ru - dolph's sto - ry done,
ding a ching a d ding ding a ching ding ding a ching a d ding
Alto only
Frost - y, he might melt in the sun.
Frost - y the Snow - man, he might melt in the sun.
Frost - y the Snow - man, he might melt in the sun.
ding ding a ching a d ding ding a ching, he might melt in the sun, if it's balm - y.
73

75
S A
T
B 1 B 2
B
p
mf
mp
Ding ding ching a ding_ ding a ching ding ding ching a ding_
Frost - y the Snow - man_____ knew the sun was hot that day,_ so he
Ding ding ching a ding_ ding a ching ding ding ching a ding_
Frost - y, yes, I'm talk-in' 'bout Frost - y, what a snow-dude.
ding ding ching a ding_ ding a ching ding ding ching a ding_ ding a ching
said, "Let's run and we'll have some fun_ now, be - fore I melt a-way."_
ding ding ching a ding_ ding a ching ding ding ching a ding_ ding a ching
Ding ding ching a ding_ ding a ching ding ding ching a ding_ ding a ching
77

S
A
ding ding ching a ding_ ding a ching ding ding ching a ding_
T
Down to the vil - lage,___ with a broom-stick in his hand,_ run-ning
B 1
B 2
ding ding ching a ding_ ding a ching ding ding ching a ding_
mp
B
Yes, I'm talk-in' 'bout Frost - y, Why a broom-stick?
79
S
A
mp
unis.
doo doo doo doo, "Catch me if___ you can!"_
T
here and there, all a-round the square,_ say-in', "Catch me if___ you can!"_
B 1
B 2
mp
doo doo doo doo, "Catch me if___ you can!"_
B
Dm tsm dm tsm dm tsm dm tsm, "Catch me if___ you can!_ I'm the man!"
mp
81

83
Then one grog - gy Christ - mas eve, San - ta came to say,
mf
p
Oo
S
A
T
B 1
B 2
B
“Frost - y, with your snap - py feet, won’t you join my de - liv - er - y fleet?”
your snap - py feet, won’t you join my de - liv - er - y fleet?” B dm
unis.
f
85

87
S A
T
B 1
B 2
B
f
mf
Frost - y the Snow - man had to hur - ry on his way, __ but he
Doo tsoo tsoo doo tsoo tsoo, hur - ry on his way, __ tsoo tsoo
Ru - dolph the Red - nosed Rein - deer had a ver - y hap - py day,
Doo tsoo tsoo doo tsoo tsoo doo tsoo tsoo doo tsoo tsoo
dm dm dm dm dm dm dm dm
87
waved good - bye, say - ing, "Don't you cry, __ I'll be back a - gain some - day." You know
doo tsoo tsoo doo tsoo tsoo, back a - gain some - day." You know
wav - ing good - bye, he cried out, "I'll be back a - gain some - day."
doo tsoo tsoo doo tsoo tsoo doo tsoo tsoo doo tsoo tsoo
dm dm dm dm dm dm dm dm dm dm dm
89

91
S
A
Dash - er and Danc - er and Pranc - er and Vix - en,
T
Dash - er and Danc - er and Pranc - er and Vix - en,
mf
B 1
Doo tsoo tsoo doo tsoo tsoo doo tsoo tsoo doo tsoo doo
B 2
doo tsoo tsoo doo tsoo tsoo doo tsoo tsoo doo tsoo
B
dm dm dm dm dm dm dm dm dm dm dm dm dm dm
91
91
Com - et and Cu - pid and Don - ner and Blitz - en.
Com - et and Cu - pid and Don - ner and Blitz - en.
doo tsoo tsoo doo tsoo tsoo doo tsoo tsoo doo tsoo doo
doo tsoo tsoo doo tsoo tsoo doo tsoo tsoo doo tsoo
dm dm dm dm dm dm dm dm dm dm dm dm dm dm
93

S A
T
B 1
B 2
B
Frost - y and Ru - dolph, they're both out of sight. We
Frost - y and Ru - dolph, they're both out of sight. We
doo tsoo tsoo doo tsoo tsoo doo tsoo tsoo doo tsoo doo
doo tsoo tsoo doo tsoo tsoo doo tsoo tsoo doo tsoo
dm dm dm dm dm dm dm dm dm dm dm dm dm
95
97
cresc.
sing of their sto - ries this ver - y Christ - mas
sing of their sto - ries this ver - y Christ - mas
doo tsoo tsoo doo tsoo, this ver - y Christ - mas
doo tsoo tsoo doo tsoo, this ver - y mer - ry Christ - mas
dm dm dm dm dm dm dm dm dm dm dm dm dm
97

S
A
T
B 1
B 2
B
night,
Christ - mas
night,
Christ - mas
night,
Christ - mas
night,
Christ - mas
night,
Christ - mas
night,
Christ - mas
night,
Christ - mas
Dm tsm dm tsm dm tsm dm tsm dm tsm dm tsm dm tsm dm tsm
99
ff
night.
They go down in his - to - ry all right!
night.
They're in his - to - ry all right!
night.
They're in his - to - ry all right!
night.
They're in his - to - ry all right!
night.
They're down in his - to - ry all right!
dm tsm dm tsm dm tsm dm tsm,
They go down in his - to - ry all right!
101

HAVE YOURSELF A MERRY LITTLE CHRISTMAS

For SATBBB a cappella

Duration: ca. 2:45

Words and Music by HUGH MARTIN
and RALPH BLANE
Arranged by KEITH ROBERTS

DO NOT PHOTOCOPY

5
p accel.
rit.
similar rubato feel throughout
S
A
T
B 1
B 2
B
Have your - self a mer - ry lit - tle Christ - mas, let your heart be light.
5
From now on our trou - bles will be out of sight, of sight.
From now on our trou - bles will be out of sight, be out of sight.
9

13
S
A
T
B 1
B 2
B
pp
mp
Mm
Have your-self a mer-ry lit-tle Christ-mas, make the Yule-tide gay.
13
From now on our trou-bles will be miles a - way.
From now on our trou-bles will be miles a - way, be miles a -
p
mf
17

21
S
mp
Here, as in old - en days, hap - py gold - en days
A
mp
way. Here, as in old - en days, hap - py gold - en days
T
mp
way. Here, as in old - en days, hap - py gold - en days
B 1
mf
Here we are as in old - en days, hap - py gold - en days of
B 2
mp
Dm dm dm dm dm dm dm dm dm dm dm dm dm dm dm dm dm dm
B
mp
way. Dm dm dm dm dm dm
21
mp
21
of yore. Friends who are dear to us
of yore. Friends who are dear to us
of yore. Friends who are dear to us
yore. Faith - ful friends who are dear to us gath - er
dm dm dm dm dm dm dm dm dm dm dm dm dm dm dm dm dm dm dm dm
dm dm dm dm dm dm
24

29
S
A
T
B 1
B 2
B
gath - er near to us once more.
Through the years we
near to us once more.
dm dm dm dm dm dm dm dm dm dm dm dm dm,
dm dm dm dm,
27
cresc. poco a poco
all will be to - geth - er, if the fates al - low.
But 'til then we'll
30

37
S
A
T
B 1
B 2
B
cresc.
mf
have to mud-dle through some - how. So have your-self a
cresc.
mer - ry lit - tle Christ - mas now, so
mer - ry lit - tle Christ - mas, have your - self a mer - ry lit - tle Christ - mas,
34
38

43 A tempo
S
A
T
B 1
B 2
B
rit. e dim.
have your-self a mer-ry lit-tle Christ-mas now.
have your-self a mer-ry lit-tle Christ-mas Oo
41
45
rit.
Mm
Oo

IT CAME UPON THE MIDNIGHT CLEAR

For SATBBB a cappella

Duration: ca. 4:10

Words by
EDMUND H. SEARS

Traditional English Melody
Adapted by Arthur Sullivan
Arranged by ROBERT RICE

S
A
T
B 1
B 2
B
espress.
"Peace
an - gels bend - ing near the earth, to touch their harps of gold, Mm
p
Mm
5
9
The
on the earth, good - will to men from heav'n's all - gra - cious king." The
good - will to men, Mm
9
9

espress.
S
world in sol - emn__ still - ness lay, to__ hear__ the an - gels sing.
A
world in sol - emn__ still - ness lay, to hear__ the an - gels sing.
T
__ sol - emn still - ness lay, to hear the an - gels sing.
B 1
mf
__ sol - emn still - ness lay, to hear the an - gels sing. Still__
B 2
B
mf
Still
mf
13
17
mf
And__
mf
And
mf
Through the__ clo - ven skies they__ come, with peace - ful wings__ un - furled, And
through the clo - ven__ skies they come, with peace - ful wings un - furled,______
through the__ clo - ven skies they__ come, with peace - ful wings un - furled,______
17
17

S
still their heav'n - ly mu - sic floats o'er all the wea - ry world. A -
A
still their heav'n - ly mu - sic floats o'er all the world.
T
still their heav'n - ly mu - sic floats, all the wea - ry
B 1
mu - sic floats o'er all the wea - ry world. A -
B 2
B
Mm
mp
21
25
S
bove its sad and low - ly plains they bend on hov - 'ring
A
Mm They
T
world. Mm
B 1
bove its sad and low - ly plains they bend on hov - 'ring
B 2
They
B
25

S
wing, and ev - er o'er its Ba - bel sounds
A
bend on hov - 'ring wing, and o'er its Ba - bel sounds
T
on hov - 'ring wing, its Ba - bel sounds
B 1
wing, and ev - er o'er its Ba - bel sounds
B 2
bend on hov - 'ring wing, and o'er its Ba - bel sounds
B
ev - er o'er its Ba - bel sounds
28
Mm
An - gels sing.
Mm
the bless - ed an - gels sing.
mp espress.
Mm An - gels sing. Yet
p
31

34
S
A
T
B 1
B 2
B
Oo
Oo
Oo
Oo
Oo
with the woes of sin and strife the world has suf - fered long. Be -
34
neath the an - gel strain have rolled two thou - sand years of wrong. And
And
And
And
34
38

42
S
A
T
B 1
B 2
B
cresc.
the love - song which they bring:
the love - song which they bring:
man, at war with man, hears not the love - song which they bring:
man, at war with man, hears not the love - song which they bring:
man, at war with man, hears not the love - song which they bring:
man, at war with man, hears not the love - song which they bring: "O
dim.
rit.
a tempo
pp
"Hush! Hush! Hush!" And
"Hush! Hush! Hush!"
"Hush! Hush! Hush!"
"Hush! Hush! Hush!"
"Hush! Hush! Hush!"
hush the noise, ye men of strife, and hear the an - gels sing."
46

50
distinto
ye, be - neath life's crush - ing load, whose forms are bend - ing low, Who
pp distinto
Ye, be - neath life's crush - ing load, whose forms are bend - ing low, Who
Ye, whose forms are bend - ing low, Who
S
A
T
B 1
B 2
B
toil a - long the climb - ing way with pain - ful steps and slow,
toil a - long the climb - ing way with pain - ful steps and slow, Look
p
54

58
S
A
T
B 1
B 2
B
mp
cresc.
Look
now, for glad and gold - en hours come swift - ly on the wing, Look
now, look now, look now, look now, Look
62
now, for glad and gold - en hours come swift - ly on the wing, Look
now, look now, look now, look now, Look
now, look now,

56
66
cresc.
S
now, for gold - en hours come on the wing. O
A
now, for glad and gold - en hours come swift - ly on the wing. O
T
for glad and gold - en hours come swift - ly on the wing. O
B 1
now, for gold - en hours come swift - ly on the wing. O
B 2
now, for glad and gold - en hours come swift - ly on the wing. O
B
Hours come swift-ly on the wing. O
f
66
S
rest be - side the wea - ry road and hear the an - gels sing. Oo
A
rest be - side the wea - ry road and hear the an - gels sing. Oo
T
rest be - side the wea - ry road and hear the an - gels sing. Oo
B 1
rest be - side the wea - ry road and hear the an - gels sing. Oo
B 2
rest be - side the wea - ry road and hear the an - gels sing. Oo
B
rest be - side the wea - ry road and hear the an - gels sing. Oo
mf
70
CHRISTMAS SONGBOOK

76
S
For lo, the days are has - t'ning on,
A
For lo, the days are has - t'ning on,
T
The days are has - t'ning on, by
B 1
The days are has - t'ning on, by
B 2
The days are has - t'ning on, by
B
The days are has - t'ning on, by
76
74
When, with the ev - er -
Al - le - lu - ia, When, with the ev - er -
proph - et bards fore - told, Al - le - lu - ia,
proph - et bards fore - told,
proph - et bards fore - told, Al - le - lu - ia, with the
proph - et bards fore - told, When, with the ev - er -
78

S
A
T
B 1
B 2
B
mp
cir - cling years, comes round the age of gold, When
cir - cling years, comes round the age of gold, When
cir - cling years, comes round the age of gold, Al - le - lu - ia,
When
cir - cling years, comes round the age of gold, Al - le - lu - ia,
cir - cling years, comes round the age of gold, Al - le - lu -
81
84
cresc.
peace shall o - ver all the earth its an - cient splen - dours
peace shall o - ver all the earth its an - cient splen - dours
its an - cient splen - dours
peace shall o - ver all the earth its an - cient splen - dours
ia,
84

S
mf
cresc. poco a poco
fling, And all the world give back the song which
A
mf cresc. poco a poco
fling, All the world give back the song which
T
mf
cresc. poco a poco
fling, And all the world give back the song which
B 1
mf cresc. poco a poco
fling, And all the world give back the song which
B 2
mf
cresc. poco a poco
And all the world give back the song which
B
mf cresc. poco a poco
All, all the world give back the song which
mf
cresc. poco a poco
87
f rit.
now the an - gels sing. A - men.
f rit.
now the an - gels, Al - le - lu - ia, A - men.
f rit.
now an - gels sing. A - men.
f rit.
now the an - gels, Al - le - lu - ia, A - men.
f rit.
now the an - gels, Al - le - lu - ia, A - men.
f rit.
now an - gels sing. A - men.
f rit.
90

THE FIRST NOWELL

For SATBBB a cappella

Duration: ca. 5:00

Traditional English Carol
Arranged by ROBERT RICE

S
A
T
B 1
B 2
B
mp
no - well. The
oh, sing no - well.
oh, sing no - well.
no - well.
cresc.
well, no - well.
no - well.
mp
5
9
first no - well the an - gel did say was to cer - tain poor shep - herds in
mp
was to cer - tain poor shep - herds in
p
Mm
p
Mm
9
9

S
fields as they lay, In fields where they lay keep - ing their sheep on a
A
fields as they lay, In fields where they lay keep - ing their sheep on a
T
p
Mm
B 1
B 2
mp
In fields where they lay keep - ing their sheep on a
B
Mm
12
S
17
cold win - ter's night that was so deep.
A
mp
cold win - ter's night that was so deep. No - well, no - well,
T
B 1
B 2
mp
cold win - ter's night that was so deep. No - well, no -
B
mp
No - well, no - well, no -
17
mp
15

S
A
T
B 1
B 2
B
— no-well, Born is the king, no -
king of Is - ra - el.
mp
They
well, no-well, Born is the king of Is - ra - el.
well, no-well, no - well, no-well, no-well, no -
18
21
Lo, lo, lo, lo, lo, lo, lo, lo!
well. Mm
Mm
look - ed up and saw a star shin-ing in the east, be - yond them far; And
well.
p

cresc. poco a poco
S
Lo, lo, lo, lo, lo, lo,
A
Lo, light!
T
Lo, light!
B 1
to the earth it gave great light, and so it con - tin - ued both
p cresc. poco a poco
B 2
Lo, light!
mp cresc.
B
light!
25
29
lo, light!
mf
No - well, no - well, no - well, no - well,
day and night. No - well, no - well, no - well, no - well,
28

Born is the king of Is - ra - el.
Born, king of Is - ra - el.
Born, king of Is - ra - el. And
Born, king of Is - ra - el. No - well.
Born, king of Is - ra - el. No - well.
Born, king of Is - ra - el. Mm
dim.
mp
31
34
by the light of that same star, three wise men came from
by the light of that same star, three wise men came from
by the light of that same star, three wise men came from

S
A
T
coun - try far. To seek for a king was
B 1
coun - try far. To seek for a king was
B 2
coun - try far. To seek for a king was
B
37
S
A
T
their in - tent, and to fol - low the star where - so -
B 1
their in - tent, and to fol - low the star where - so -
B 2
their in - tent, and to fol - low the star where - so -
mp
B
and to fol - low the star where - so -
39

42
S
No - well, no - well, no - well.
This
A
No - well, no - well, no - well.
T
ev - er it went. No - well, no - well, no - well.
B 1
ev - er it went. No - well.
B 2
ev - er it went Born is the king of Is - ra - el.
B
ev - er it went. Born is the king of Is - ra - el.
42

47
S
A
T
B 1
B 2
B
star drew nigh to the north-west, o'er Beth - le - hem it
Ah
Ah
Ah
Ah
Ah
p
47
took its rest, And there it did both stop and stay right
right
right
right
right
right
cresc.
50

55
f dolce
o - ver the place where Je - sus lay. No - well, no - well, no -
well, no - well,
mp
Born is the king of Is - ra - el. Then
mf
Ah
53
56

59
S
A
T
B 1
B 2
B
mf
Ah
en - tered in those wise men three, fell rev - 'rent - ly up -
en - tered in those wise men three, fell rev - 'rent - ly up -
en - tered in those wise men three, fell rev - 'rent - ly up -
mf
Ah
59
59
on their knee, And of - fered up in his pres - ence their
on their knee, And of - fered up in his pres - ence their
on their knee, And of - fered up in his pres - ence their
f
their
62

S
A
T
B 1
B 2
B
67
Lo, lo, lo, No - well, no - well, no - well.
No - well, no - well.
gold and myrrh and frank - in - cense. No - well, no - well, no - well, no -
gold and myrrh and frank - in - cense.
gold and myrrh and frank - in - cense.
gold and myrrh and frank - in - cense.
Born is the king of Is - ra - el.
mp
dim.
p
65
68

71
S
A
T
B 1
B 2
B
mf
Then
p lilting
No - well, no - well.
well,
No - well, no - well, no - well, no - well.
No - well, no - well, no - well.
No - well, no - well, no - well,
75
let us all with one ac - cord sing prais - es to our
let us all with one ac - cord sing prais - es to our
no - well. sing prais - es to our
sing prais - es to our
with one ac - cord sing prais - es to our
no - well. sing prais - es to our

S
A
T
B 1
B 2
B
heav'n - ly Lord, That hath made heav'n and earth of nought, and
heav'n - ly Lord, No - well, no - well. and
heav'n - ly Lord, and
mp
mf
78
83
with his blood man - kind hath bought.
with his blood man - kind hath bought. No - well, no - well,
with his blood man - kind hath bought. No - well,
with his blood man - kind hath bought. No - well, no -
81

S
A
T
B 1
B 2
B
dim.
no - well, Born is the king, no - well.
Born, king of Is - ra - el.
well, no - well, Born is the king of Is - ra - el.
well, no - well, no - well, no - well, no - well, no -
84
87
p
tr
rit.
Oo
well.
Oo
87

CAROL OF THE BELLS

For SATBBB a cappella

Duration: ca. 2:40

By PETER WILHOUSKY
Arranged by KEITH ROBERTS

* *Close to the "ng" where indicated with asterisks.*

7
S
A
T
B 1
B 2
B
ding*
ding*
mp
sweet sil - ver bells,
Hark how the bells, sweet sil - ver bells,
dong*
dong*
ding*
ding*
7
mp
5
all seem to say throw cares a - way. Christ - mas is here, bring - ing good cheer
dong*
ding*
8

mp
Ding dong ding dong, that is their song,
ding*
to young and old, meek and the bold.
Ding dong ding dong
dong*
Ding dong
ding*
Ding dong
10
13
with joy-ful ring all car-ol-ing.
Ding dong ding dong
ding dong ding dong,
One seems to hear words of good cheer
ding dong,
Ding dong,
12
S
A
T
B 1
B 2
B
p

S
A
T
B 1
B 2
B
mf
ding dong ding dong, Oh, how they pound, rais - ing the sound
from ev - 'ry - where, fill - ing the air. Oh, how they pound, rais - ing the sound
from ev - 'ry - where, fill - ing the air. Ding dong ding dong
from ev - 'ry - where, fill - ing the air. Ding dong
from ev - 'ry - where, fill - ing the air. Ding dong
Ding dong
14
17
f
o'er hill and dale, tell - ing their tale. Gai - ly they ring while peo - ple sing
o'er hill and dale, tell - ing their tale. Gai - ly they ring while peo - ple sing
ding dong ding dong, Gai - ly they ring while peo - ple sing
ding dong, Gai - ly they ring, Dong,
ding dong, Ding dong,
ding dong, Ding dong
16

S
A
T
B 1
B 2
B
songs of good cheer, Christ - mas is here. Gai - ly they ring while peo - ple sing
songs of good cheer, Christ - mas is here. Gai - ly they ring while peo - ple sing
songs of good cheer Christ - mas is here. Gai - ly they ring while peo - ple sing
songs of good cheer, Christ - mas is here. Gai - ly they ring, Dong,
songs of good cheer, Christ - mas is here. Ding dong,
ding, Christ - mas is here. Dong
18
21
songs of good cheer, Christ - mas is here.
songs of good cheer, Christ - mas is here. Mer - ry, mer - ry, mer - ry, mer - ry Christ - mas.
songs of good cheer, Christ - mas is here,
songs of good cheer, Christ - mas is here.
songs of good cheer, Christ - mas is here. Mer - ry, mer - ry, mer - ry, mer - ry Christ - mas.
ding, Christ - mas is here,
21
20

S
A
T
B 1
B 2
B
f
dim.
Mer - ry, mer - ry, mer - ry Christ - mas. On, on they send, on with - out end,
mf
Mer - ry, mer - ry, mer - ry, mer - ry Christ - mas. Oo Ah
here. Ding dong ding dong
Mer - ry, mer - ry, mer - ry Christ - mas. On, on they send, on with - out end,
Mer - ry, mer - ry, mer - ry, mer - ry Christ - mas. Oo Ah
here. Oo Ah
22
25
mp
p
their joy - ful tone to ev - 'ry home. On with - out end, Ding*
Oo Ah, Ding* ding*
ding dong ding dong, Dong* dong*
their joy - ful tone to ev - 'ry home. Ding* ng*
Oo Ah Oo
Oo Ah Oo
24

S
A
T
B 1
B 2
B
29
pp
ding* Ding ding,
ding* Ding ding,
dong* Dong, dong,
mf
p
Ding dong ding dong ding dong ding dong,
Ding dong ding dong ding dong ding dong,
cresc.
Bong bong bong bong,
27
33
Hark how the bells, sweet sil - ver bells, all seem to say throw cares a - way.
mp
Ding dong ding dong
Ding dong ding dong
Hark how the bells, sweet sil - ver bells, all seem to say throw cares a - way.
Bong bong
Bong bong

S
A
T
B 1
B 2
B
Christ - mas is here, bring - ing good cheer to young and old, meek and the bold.
ding dong ding dong,
ding dong ding dong,
Christ - mas is here, bring - ing good cheer to young and old, meek and the bold.
bong bong,
bong bong,
35
37
mp
Ding dong ding dong ding dong ding dong
Ding dong ding dong ding dong ding dong
Ding dong ding dong, that is their song, with joy - ful ring all car - ol - ing.
Ding dong ding dong ding dong ding dong
p
Ding dong,
Ding dong ding dong
37

S
A
T
B 1
B 2
B
cresc.
mp cresc.
ding dong ding dong ding dong ding dong,
One seems to hear words of good cheer from ev-'ry-where, fill - ing the air.
One seems to hear songs of good cheer from ev-'ry-where, fill - ing the air.
ding dong ding dong
39
mf
ding dong ding dong ding dong ding dong ding dong ding dong,
Ding dong ding dong ding dong ding dong ding dong ding dong,
Oh, how they pound, rais - ing the sound o'er hill and dale, tell - ing their tale.
ding dong ding dong,
41

43
f
S
Gai - ly they ring while peo - ple sing songs of good cheer, Christ - mas is here.
A
Gai - ly they ring while peo - ple sing songs of good cheer, Christ - mas is here.
T
Gai - ly they ring while peo - ple sing songs of good cheer, Christ - mas is here.
B 1
Ding dong ding dong ding dong ding dong
B 2
Ding dong ding dong ding dong ding dong
B
Ding dong ding, Christ - mas is
43
S
Gai - ly they ring while peo - ple sing songs of good cheer, Christ - mas is here.
A
Gai - ly they ring while peo - ple sing songs of good cheer, Christ - mas is here.
T
Gai - ly they ring while peo - ple sing songs of good cheer, Christ - mas is,
B 1
ding dong ding dong ding dong ding dong,
B 2
ding dong ding dong ding dong ding dong,
B
here. Dong ding, Christ - mas is
45

47
S
A
T
B 1
B 2
B
mf
Ding ding,
Dong dong,
Ding ding,
Dong ding-a-dong dong ding-a-dong-a
f
Mer-ry, mer-ry, mer-ry, mer-ry Christ-mas. Mer-ry, mer-ry, mer-ry, mer-ry Christ-mas.
here, Christ-mas is here, Christ-mas is
47
f
dim.
51
mp
On, on they send, on with-out end, their joy-ful tone to ev-'ry home. On with-out end,
p
Ding dong ding dong ding dong ding dong, Ding dong
Ding dong ding dong ding dong ding dong, Ding dong
Ding dong ding dong ding dong ding dong, Ding dong
On, on they send, on with-out end, their joy-ful tone to ev-'ry home. Ding dong
here. Oo Ah Oo Ah Oo
49

S
A
T
B 1
B 2
B
pp
p
Ding* ding* ding*
ding dong, Ding* ding* ding*
ding dong, Ding* dong* dong*
ding dong, Ding* ding* ding*
ding dong, Ding* dong ding dong dong ding dong,
Bong bong bong bong bong bong bong bong,
cresc.
52
57
mp
mf
Ding* ding* ding dong
Ding* ding* ding dong
Dong* dong* dong*
Ding* ding* ding dong ding-a-dong
Dong ding dong dong ding dong, ding ding-a-dong*
Bong bong bong bong bong bong
57

61
sub. p
S
ding dong, Ding dong
sub. mp
A
ding ding dong, Hark how the bells, sweet sil - ver bells,
sub. p
T
ding___ dong, Ding ding - a - ding - a - dong
sub. p
B 1
dong ding - a - dong, Ding dong
sub. p
B 2
ding ding - a - dong,* ___ Ding ding
sub. p
B
bong bong, Bong
61
sub. p
60
S
ding dong ding dong
A
all seem to say throw cares a - way. Christ - mas is here, bring - ing good cheer
T
ding dong ding - a - ding - a - dong ding - a - ding - a - dong
B 1
ding ding - a - ding - a - dong, Mer - ry, mer - ry, mer - ry
B 2
ding - a - ding - a - dong dong, Mer - ry, mer - ry, mer - ry Christ - mas.
B
bong bong
62

S
A
T
B 1
B 2
B
mp
p
ding, Mer - ry, mer - ry, mer - ry, Ding dong ding dong, that is their song,
to young and old, meek and the bold. Ding dong ding dong
ding - a - ding - a - dong ding - a - ding - a - dong, Ding dong
Christ - mas. Mer - ry, mer - ry, mer - ry, Ding dong
Mer - ry, mer - ry, mer - ry Christ - mas.
bong,
64
67
with joy - ful ring all car - ol - ing. Mer - ry, mer - ry, mer - ry
ding dong ding dong, One seems to hear words of good cheer
ding dong, One seems to hear words of good cheer
ding dong, One seems to hear words of good cheer
Ding dong, One seems to hear words of good cheer
Mer - ry, mer - ry, mer - ry, mer - ry Christ - mas.
66

S
A
T
B 1
B 2
B
mf
Christ - mas. Mer - ry, mer - ry, mer - ry, Oh, how they pound, rais - ing the sound
from ev - 'ry - where, fill - ing the air. Oh, how they pound, rais - ing the sound
from ev - 'ry - where, fill - ing the air. Ding dong ding dong
from ev - 'ry - where, fill - ing the air. Ding ding ding dong,
from ev - 'ry - where, fill - ing the air. Ding ding ding dong,
Mer - ry, mer - ry, mer - ry, mer - ry Christ - mas. Ding ding dong
68
71
f
o'er hill and dale, tell - ing their tale. Ah, while peo - ple sing
o'er hill and dale, tell - ing their tale. Gai - ly they ring while peo - ple sing
ding, Mer - ry, mer - ry, mer - ry, Gai - ly they ring while peo - ple sing
Mer - ry, mer - ry, mer - ry, mer - ry, mer - ry, mer - ry, Gai - ly they ring, Dong,
Mer - ry, mer - ry, mer - ry Christ - mas. Ding dong,
ding dong, Ding dong
70

S
A
T
B 1
B 2
B
songs of good cheer, Christ - mas is here. Ah, while peo - ple sing
songs of good cheer, Christ - mas is here. Gai - ly they ring while peo - ple sing
songs of good cheer, Mer - ry, mer - ry, mer - ry, Gai - ly they ring while peo - ple sing
songs of good cheer, Mer - ry, mer - ry, mer - ry, Gai - ly they ring, Dong,
songs of good cheer, Christ - mas is here. Ding dong
ding, Christ - mas is here. Dong
72
75
songs of good cheer, Christ - mas is here. Mer - ry, mer - ry, mer - ry, mer - ry Christ - mas.
songs of good cheer, Christ - mas is here. Mer - ry, mer - ry, mer - ry, mer - ry Christ - mas.
songs of good cheer, Mer - ry, mer - ry, mer - ry, Mer - ry, mer - ry, mer - ry, mer - ry Christ - mas.
songs of good cheer, Mer - ry, mer - ry, mer - ry, Mer - ry, mer - ry, mer - ry, mer - ry Christ - mas.
songs of good cheer, Christ - mas is here. Mer - ry, mer - ry, mer - ry, mer - ry Christ - mas.
ding, Christ - mas is here.
75
74

sub. p
Mer - ry, mer - ry, mer - ry, mer - ry Christ - mas.
f
dim.
On, on they send, on with - out end,
mf
Oo Ah
Ding dong ding dong
Mer - ry, mer - ry, mer - ry, mer - ry Christ - mas.
Oo Ah
76
their joy - ful tone to ev - 'ry home.
79
mp
On with - out end,
Oo Ah,
Ding*
ding dong ding dong,
Dong*
Ding*
Oo Ah Oo
78

S
A
T
B 1
B 2
B
p
pp
Ding*
ding*
ding*
ding*
dong*
dong*
ng*
80
On with - out end.
82

From the Motion Picture Irving Berlin's HOLIDAY INN

WHITE CHRISTMAS

For SATBBB a cappella

Duration: ca. 3:00

Words and Music by IRVING BERLIN
Arranged by ROBERT RICE

S
A
T
B 1
B 2
B
mp
dah dot dot dot dot dot doo dop
doo doo dah dah dot dot dot dot dot doo dop
bee doo bee dah dot dot dot dot dot doo dop
doo doo dah dah dot dot dot dot dot doo dop
doo dop ching-a ching ching-a
4
9
p
I'm dream-ing of a white Christ-mas,
ching ching ching, oh, Dm dm dm dm dm dm dm dm dm dm dm dm dm dm dm
R.H.
8

S
A
T
B 1
B 2
B
pp
Oo
pp
Oo
just like the ones I used to know,
where the
dm dm dm dm dm dm dm dm dm b dm b dm b dm b dm dm
pp
pp
13
17
pp
where the tree - tops glis - ten, Oo chil - dren lis - ten
where the tree - tops glis - ten, Oo chil - dren lis - ten
where the tree - tops glis - ten, Oo chil - dren lis - ten
tree - tops glis - ten and chil - dren lis - ten to hear
pp
where the tree - tops glis - ten, Oo chil - dren lis - ten
Dm tsm dm tsm dm tsm dm tsm dm tsm dm tsm dm tsm dm tsm
17
17

S
to hear sleigh bells in, ching-a ching ching-a ching ching ding, oh,
A
to hear sleigh bells in, ching-a ching ching-a ching ching ding, oh,
T
to hear sleigh bells in, ching-a ching ching-a ching ching ding, oh,
B 1
sleigh bells in the snow.
B 2
to hear sleigh bells in, ching-a ching ching-a ching ching ding, oh,
B
b dm b dm b dm b dm b dm b dm b dm oh,
21
25
p
cresc.
3
S
I'm dream - ing of a white Christ - mas
A
I'm dream - ing of a white Christ - mas
T
I'm dream - ing of a white Christ - mas
B 1
I'm dream - ing of a white Christ - mas
B 2
I'm dream - ing of a white Christ - mas
B
Dm tsm dm tsm dm tsm dm tsm dm tsm dm tsm dm tsm dm doo dah,

S
A
T
B 1
B 2
B
with ev - 'ry Christ - mas card I write.
with ev - 'ry Christ - mas card I write.
with ev - 'ry Christ - mas card I write. May your
with ev - 'ry Christ - mas card I write. May your
with ev - 'ry Christ - mas card I write. May your
with ev - 'ry Christ - mas card I write. Tsm dm tsm dm tsm dm tsm
p
mp
29
33
mer - ry, your days be mer - ry and bright,
mer - ry, your days be mer - ry and bright,
days be mer - ry, mer - ry, may your days be mer - ry and bright,
days be mer - ry, mer - ry, may your days be mer - ry and bright,
days be mer - ry and bright and may
B dm b dm dm tsm dm tsm dm tsm dm tsm dm tsm dm tsm

S
all your Christ - mas - es be white.
A
all your Christ - mas - es be white.
T
all your Christ - mas - es be white.
B 1
all your Christ - mas - es be white.
B 2
all your Christ - mas - es be white.
mf
The
B
b dm b dm b dm b dm ching - a ching ching - a ching
mp
37
41
mp
Mm
Mm
Mm
Mm
sun is shin - ing, the grass is green, the or - ange and palm trees sway. There's
Dm dm dm dm dm dm dm dm dm dm dm
41

S
A
T
B 1
B 2
B
Oo
nev - er been such a
day,
no
way.
Oo
no
way.
Oo
nev - er been such a
day,
no
way.
nev - er been such
a day
in
Bev - er - ly
Hills,
L. A.
Oo
no
way.
45
49
p
Oo
mp
But it's De - cem - ber the twen - ty - fourth,
p
Oo
Oo
Oo
p
Oo
Oo
p
Oo
p
Oo
doo doo doo doo doo doo
49
p
49

S
A
and I am long - ing to be up north.
T
Oo doo doo ching - a ching ching - a ching ching ching, oh
B 1
doo, long - ing to be up north. ching ching ching, oh
B 2
doo doo doo doo ching - a ching ching - a ching ching ching, oh
B
doo doo doo doo doo oh
53
57
mf
dah dah doo dn doo dah doo dah dah doo dn doo bee doo bee doo doo
mp
doo dah doo dah dah dah doo dn doo dah
doo dah doo dah doo dah
doo dah doo dah doo dah
Dm tsm dm tsm dm tsm dm tsm dm tsm dm tsm
57

S
A
T
B 1
B 2
B
mf
dah dah doo dn doo dah dah dah d-dl oo dah
doo bee doo bee doo doo bee doo doo doo bee doo dah dah dah doo wah
doo dah dah doo dn doo doo doo bee doo dah dah dah doo wah
doo dah doo dah doo dah doo dah
doo dah doo dah doo dah doo dah
dm tsm dm tsm dm tsm dm tsm dm tsm dm tsm
60
65
p
doo doo dah Oo doo
bee doo wah bee doo wah doo doo dah Oo doo doo
bee doo wah doo doo dah Oo doo doo
mf
Doo bee doo doo bee doo bee
doo doo doo dah Oo doo doo
doo bee doo bee doo bee doo bee doo doo Dm tsm dm tsm
63

S
A
T
B 1
B 2
B
cresc.
doo doo doo doo doo doo doo doo doo
doo doo doo doo doo doo doo doo doo doo
doo doo doo doo doo doo doo doo doo doo
doo dn doo doo bee d doo doo dn doo bah doo doo doo bee doo wah
doo doo doo doo doo doo doo doo doo doo
dm tsm dm tsm dm tsm dm tsm dm tsm dm tsm
66
doo doo doo doo dah
doo doo doo doo doo doo doo bee doo doo bee
doo doo doo doo doo doo doo bee doo doo bee
bee doo wah bee doo bee doo doo doo d-dl doo dah doo bee doo doo bee
doo doo doo doo doo doo doo bee doo doo bee
dm tsm dm tsm dm tsm dm b dm b dm
69

73
S
A
T
B 1
B 2
B
mf
f
cresc.
oh, I'm dream - ing of a
doo doo dah, oh, I'm dream - ing of a
b dm, oh, I'm, I'm a - dream - ing, yes, I'm a - dream - ing,
white Christ - mas with ev - 'ry
dream - ing of a ver - y white Christ - mas with ev - 'ry, ev - 'ry
72
75

mp cresc.
S
Christ - mas card I write. May your
A
Christ - mas card I write. May your
T
Christ - mas card I write. May your
B 1
Christ - mas card I write. May your
B 2
Christ - mas card I write. May your
B
Christ - mas card I write, ev - 'ry card I write.
78
81
days be mer - ry and bright, your days be
days be mer - ry and bright,
days be mer - ry, mer - ry and bright, your days be
days be mer - ry, mer - ry and bright, may your days be
days be mer - ry, mer - ry and bright, your days be
B dm b dm, mer - ry, mer - ry and bright, may your days be

S
A
T
B 1
B 2
B
mf cresc.
mer - ry and bright, your days be mer - ry and bright,
be mer - ry, mer - ry and bright,
mer - ry and bright, your days be mer - ry, mer - ry and bright,
mer - ry and bright, your days be mer - ry, mer - ry and bright,
mer - ry and bright, your days be mer - ry, mer - ry and bright,
mer - ry and bright, your, B dm b dm b dm, mer - ry and bright,
84
ff
89
may all your
be mer - ry and bright, may all your
your days be mer - ry and bright, may all your
your days be mer - ry and bright, may all your
may your days be mer - ry and bright, may all your
may your days be mer - ry and bright, may, Dm tsm dm tsm
87

S
A
T
B 1
B 2
B
Christ-mas-es, may all your Christ-mas-es, may all your mer-ry
dm tsm dm b dm tsm dm tsm dm tsm dm b tsm b dm b dm
90
Christ - mas - es be white!
Christ - mas - es, Doo bee doo doo bee doo, be white!
Doo, be white!
b dm dm, be white!
94

SILENT NIGHT

For SATBBB a cappella

Duration: ca. 4:15

Words by JOSEPH MOHR

Music by FRANZ X. GRUBER
Arranged by KEITH ROBERTS

6 Faster (♩. = ca. 42)
S
A
T
B 1
B 2
B
Oo
Oo
Oo
Si - lent night, ho - ly night. All is calm,
Oo
6 Faster (♩. = ca. 42)
5
Oo
Mm
Oo
Oo
Oo
all is bright, round yon vir - gin moth - er and child.
Oo
Oo
Oo
Oo
9

S
A
T
B 1
B 2
B
Mm
Oo
Oo
Oo
Ho - ly in - fant, so ten - der and mild, sleep in heav - en - ly peace,
Oo
Oo
Oo
Oo
Oo
Oo
12
17
Tempo I
poco rit.
p
Oo
Oo
Oo
sleep in heav - en - ly peace.
Oo
16

S
A
T
B 1
B 2
B
mp
rit.
Oo
p
22
Slower (♩. = ca. 30)
Si - lent night,
ho - ly night.
Shep - herds quake
mf
cresc.
19
22

S
at the sight.
Ah
Ah
A
at the sight.
Ah
Ah
T
at the sight.
Ah
Ah
B 1
Oo
Ah
B 2
Oo
Glo - ries stream from heav - en a - far,
Oo
Glo - ries stream from heav - en a - far,
25
Al - le - lu - ia,
Al - le - lu - ia.
Christ, the Sav - iour, is
Al - le - lu - ia,
Al - le - lu - ia.
Ah
Ah
Ah
Ah
Ah
Ah
heav'n - ly hosts sing Al - le - lu - ia.
Ah
heav'n - ly hosts sing Al - le - lu - ia.
Ah
28

S
A
T
B 1
B 2
B
poco rit.
33 Tempo I
born,
Christ, the Sav - iour, is born.
mf
Ah
Oo
f
a tempo
mp
Mm
31
34

38 (Tempo I)
S
A
T
B 1
B 2
B
mp
Si - lent night, ho - ly night. Son of God,
Son of God,
Si - lent night, ho - ly night. Son of God,
Si - lent night, ho - ly night. Son of God,
Si - lent night, ho - ly night. Son of God,
Si - lent night, ho - ly night. Son of God,
38 (Tempo I)
38
love's pure light. Ra - diant beams from thy ho - ly face,
love's pure light. Ra - diant beams, thy ho - ly face,
love's pure light. Ra - diant beams, ho - ly face,
love's pure light. Ra - diant beams from thy ho - ly face,
love's pure light. Ra - diant beams, ho - ly face,
love's pure light. Ra - diant beams, ho - ly face,
41

S
A
T
B 1
B 2
B
cresc.
mf
with the dawn of re - deem - ing grace, Je - sus,
with the dawn, re - deem - ing grace, Je - sus,
with the dawn, re - deem - ing grace, Je - sus, Lord, at thy
with the dawn of re - deem - ing grace, Je - sus, Lord, at thy
with the dawn, re - deem - ing grace, Je - sus, Lord, at thy
with the dawn, re - deem - ing grace, Je - sus, Lord,
44
poco rit.
rit.
dim.
Lord, at thy birth, Je - sus, Lord, at thy
at thy birth, Je - sus, Je - sus, Lord, at thy...
birth, Je - sus, Je - sus, Lord, at thy...
birth, Je - sus, Lord, at thy...
birth, Je - sus, Je - sus, Lord, at thy...
at thy birth, Je - sus, Je - sus, Lord, at thy...
47

50 Slower (♩. = ca. 30)
S
A
T
B 1
B 2
B
mp
birth.
Oo
Mm
rit.
p
dim.
50
53